The author's thanks to Dr. E. A. Speiser of the University of Pennsylvania and Dr. C. H. Gordon of Brandeis University for their helpful advice concerning the manuscript of this book; to Dr. Edward B. Danson of the Museum of Northern Arizona and James Ford of the American Museum of Natural History for their suggestions on American Indian cultures; and to Dr. Moshe Dothan and General Yigael Yadin for the opportunity to take part in two "digs" in Israel.

The plan of the Jarmo expedition house on page 29 and the preliminary sketches of typical Jarmo antiquities on page 31 are taken from *Digging Across the Tigris,* by Linda Braidwood, and are used by courtesy of the Oriental Institute of the University of Chicago; the diagram of Stonehenge in its third phase on page 11 is from *The Testimony of the Spade,* by Geoffrey Bibby, and is used by permission of Alfred A. Knopf, Inc.; the drawing of the Corn Spirit on page 59 is from *Magic Books of Mexico,* and is used by permission of Penguin Books, Ltd. The drawing of Tepe Gawra on page 17 is adapted from a photograph by courtesy of Dr. E. A. Speiser.

The passage from the *Iliad* on page 22 is taken from Homer's *Iliad,* translated by E. V. Rieu, and published by Penguin Books, Inc., Baltimore, Maryland; the quotation on page 42 is from *From the Tablets of Sumer,* by Samuel Noah Kramer, published by The Falcon's Wing Press.

THE FIRST BOOK OF
ARCHAEOLOGY

By
NORA BENJAMIN KUBIE

ILLUSTRATED BY THE AUTHOR

FRANKLIN WATTS, INC.
575 LEXINGTON AVENUE
NEW YORK 22, N. Y.

History From Things

Somewhere in a desert where only the wandering tribesman passes, there is a mound of earth underneath which lies the palace of a long-dead king. Somewhere in a steaming jungle where monkeys swing among the vines, there is the forgotten temple of a once powerful god. And somewhere under the sands of a now barren river valley there lies a village where, long ago, ordinary people lived ordinary lives. One of these days an archaeologist will explore these lost places, study them, and tell the rest of us about the vanished men who built them.

"Archaio" is the Greek word for "ancient." Archaeology is the study of how people lived in ancient times, the history of ancient man from the *things* he left behind: his house, his tools, his pots and pans; his burials; records written in his own words.

2

Written history, including the earliest written records, covers patchily only about the past five thousand years — perhaps a hundredth of the period which modern archaeologists study. Man probably appeared on earth about half a million years ago. Behind each of us there stretches a long line of people — our ancestors — going back to man's earliest days. From archaeology we can learn about these ancestors of ours, of whom we could hear in no other way. Most of us are interested in what the other fellow is like, even though he may have lived centuries ago.

Often the things that belonged to ancient man are buried under the dust of many thousand years, and must be excavated — that is, dug up. That is why an archaeological expedition is called a "dig." Field archaeology — the discovery and exploration of ancient remains — is "history in the open air."

The Road To Nineveh

The early archaeologists were amateurs who had many adventures. Here is the story of a great Englishman, Austen Henry Layard. As a boy, young Austen read every book about travel in the East that he could find. His favorite book was *The Arabian Nights* — tales of the "Thousand and One Nights" of the wonderful city of Baghdad on the Tigris.

One day of pouring rain in the year 1840, the doorkeeper of the British Consulate in Damascus, Syria, was astonished to hear a

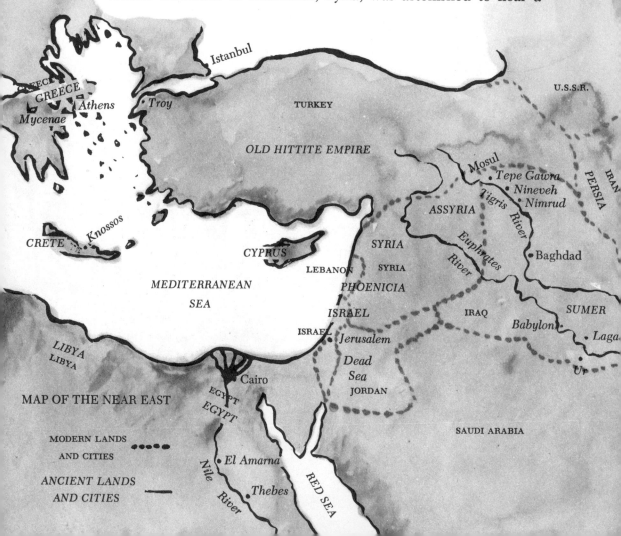

MAP OF THE NEAR EAST

MODERN LANDS
AND CITIES ••••

ANCIENT LANDS
AND CITIES ——

ragged young man, filthy and burned black by the sun, ask for the consul in educated English. It was Layard, who, at the age of twenty-two, had put his small savings in his pocket, left his law clerk's job in London, and set out for a job in Ceylon. But he never reached it, for he fell in love with Syria, Persia, and Mesopotamia — the land between the Tigris and Euphrates Rivers.

He had come to Damascus from Palestine, camping in the tents of wandering Bedouin tribes, sleeping native style on a carpet he carried on the back of his horse. In a lonely ravine he was attacked by Arab bandits, but he held his gun to the chieftain's head and boldly bluffed the robbers into letting him go. Later he was again attacked and stripped of everything but his trousers, shirt, and tattered Arab cloak. It was so he arrived in Damascus, on foot and penniless. But he was not discouraged. He was soon on his way to visit the city of Mosul in Mesopotamia, and the earthen mounds nearby. According to the local Arabs, they covered the site of Nineveh, capital of ancient Assyria.

Layard had read in the Bible of Nineveh, "that great city." Many prophets had cried out against its wickedness, and foretold that it would be laid waste, to become "a desolation and dry like the wilderness." And so it happened, almost 2,500 years ago. In Austen Layard's time Mesopotamia was ruled by corrupt Turkish pashas. The countryside around Mosul was indeed dry and desolate. In the old days, legend had it, the Garden of Eden had flourished in this valley. But for five thousand years rival peoples — Sumerians, Babylonians, Assyrians, Persians, Greeks, Arabs, Turks — had fought over the once rich land. They had left it scorched and broken, dotted with heaps of earth which had once been big cities. No one knew for sure which one of the mounds, if any, was Nineveh.

Layard became friendly with the French consul at Mosul, Paul Émile Botta. Then he wandered on through Mesopotamia and Persia, studying ruins, meeting robbers every few days, but also making friends with the wildest of the local tribes. Layard visited Mosul again in 1842 and found Botta busy digging into the mound of Kuyunjik. It was the first time anyone had attempted to excavate an Assyrian mound.

Botta got no quick results, and soon moved to nearby Khorsabad where, a villager told him, there were sculptures. Within a few days his workmen uncovered a building of more than a hundred rooms, which proved to be the palace of mighty Sargon II, the ruler of Assyria from 722 to 705 B.C. Before Botta's discovery the Assyrians had been heard of only vaguely as a people feared and hated by the Biblical Hebrews. From out the earth the Assyrian kings now rose, carved in stone, with tall turbans, carefully

Assyrians charging the enemy   (British Museum)   6

curled beards, and long, richly patterned robes. Their palace doorways were guarded by sculptured monsters with the bodies of bulls or lions, wings, and the heads of men.

Layard longed to try his hand at digging, too. There were many delays. But finally, one night when he was sleeping in the tent of a sheik, he received letters from Mosul. And by the light of a camel-dung fire he read the permit from Turkish authorities which allowed him to begin excavations.

He rode out to the great mound of Nimrud, some miles down the Tigris from Mosul, and hired six workmen. In his book, *Nineveh and Its Remains*, Layard describes how they yelled and capered like madmen as the work went deeper and deeper into the ruined passageways beneath the surface of the mound. Layard had discovered the palace of King Ashurnasirpal II, built in the ninth century B.C. The walls were sculptured with horsemen, chariots, battles, sieges, captives bringing gifts of earrings, bracelets, and monkeys. When the colossal human head of a winged lion appeared from the earth, the workmen cried out that it was a

King Ashurnasirpal II and his attendants
(Metropolitan Museum)

godlike hero from the most ancient of days, "Nimrod the Mighty Hunter," himself! This was but one of many such giants that were painfully dragged from the excavations with ropes and rollers and manpower, and sent off to the British Museum in London.

Later, at Kuyunjik, Layard renewed the work that Botta had given up too soon, and found the palace of Sennacherib, a dreaded Assyrian conqueror to whom a large part of the world paid tribute in the seventh century B.C. There was no longer any doubt that at Kuyunjik, Layard and Botta, between them, had discovered the royal palaces of Nineveh, "that great city."

Removing a winged monster at Nimrud

(From Layard's Nineveh and Its Remains)

How Archaeology Grew

In two years' work Layard discovered eight Assyrian palaces and shipped hundreds of tons of sculpture to England. He and Botta were pioneers; their methods were self-taught and crude. In their haste they broke many things of value and paid no attention to common objects of ordinary use which today's archaeologists would be seeking.

Archaeology grew slowly as a science. Modern archaeology is only a little over a hundred years old.

Between ancient times and our own a curtain of ignorance once dropped. After Rome fell to the barbarians in the fifth century, Europe entered the Dark Ages, when few people dared to travel, and fewer still could read and write. The monasteries preserved some Greek, Roman, and Hebrew accounts of the ancient world, and a handful of scholars knew them. The Moslem Arabs at this time built an empire from Arabia to Spain. The old histories translated into Arabic could be read at Moslem universities by the few Christian and Jewish students. But for most Europeans the Bible was the only book, and, taken as exact truth, it gave rise to some rather strange ideas about history and geography.

Then gradually the curtain began to lift. The Crusaders went to Palestine, land of the Bible. Merchants dared to travel again. The ancient great powers had disappeared, but ruins remained to suggest their story.

With the Italian Renaissance in the sixteenth century came a reborn enthusiasm for art and learning. Greek and Latin were again read. Statues long buried in Italian gardens were dug up and eagerly collected. Those who loved ancient art were called the "dilettanti." A "Society of Dilettanti" was formed in England in 1733. From the fad for collecting "antiquities," and with the help of history, the science of archaeology was born in the mid-nineteenth century. Today it is still opening windows on our past.

Beginnings In England

To this day many English schoolboys spend their holidays digging up Roman walls and the barrows, or graves, of the ancient Britons. The very first antiquarian society was founded in the reign of Queen Elizabeth I; and her successor, King James I, sent his architect to make an examination of Stonehenge, a great circle of upright stones which had stood on Salisbury Plain since pre-historic times. Some of the huge blocks were of native sandstone, but others, the "blue stones," could have been quarried nowhere in the neighborhood. Most of the stone lintels which roofed the outer circle in a continuous ring have fallen now, and so have a pair of standing stones twenty-two feet high, which towered above a flat stone thought to be an altar. But Stonehenge is still an awesome sight, and there can be little wonder that many strange stories were told about it. Some said that Merlin, the wizard of King Arthur's court, had brought it bodily from Ireland by his magic. The antiquarians thought it the temple of a mysterious Celtic priesthood, the druids.

Modern excavators have dug up most, but not all, of the facts about Stonehenge. It was rebuilt three times; pottery and the flint

Stonehenge

tools of the builders have been found. It was always a temple of sun worship. A line drawn from the "altar" to a stone known since earliest times as the "hele" (sun) stone points directly at the rising sun on Midsummer Day. Or it did, more exactly, some time between 1900 and 1500 B.C. The quarry from which the blue stones came was located in Wales, a hundred and fifty miles away. How they were transported such a distance in those far-off times seems as magical as if Merlin really did have a part in it.

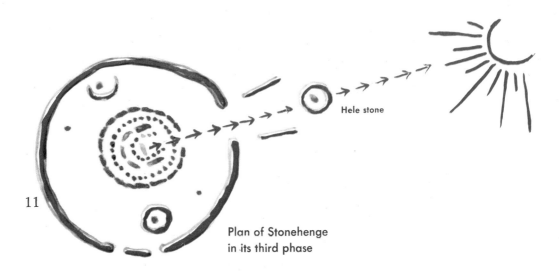

11

Hele stone

Plan of Stonehenge
in its third phase

Beginnings In Italy

In 1738 the Queen of Naples sent an officer of the Royal Engineers to hunt for more of the lovely statues that had been found at the foot of the nearby volcano Vesuvius. He found the statues, but the excavators who followed him found something much more important: buried cities.

The gay Roman resorts of Pompeii and Herculaneum had been destroyed by the eruption of Vesuvius in A.D. 79. Eyewitnesses who escaped wrote down the story. On the fatal day, people were going about their business, shopping, doing housework, when the sky darkened and ashes began to fall. Those who waited to find their families or collect their valuables were trapped. Under the volcanic lava and ash they lay as they had fallen, holding their children by the hand, with their pet dogs nearby. Houses stood upright; pots were on the kitchen table; wineshops and public baths were ready for customers. So we know exactly what life was like in a Roman town of the first century A.D. Lava and ash have preserved the record perfectly.

Mosaic from Pompeii
(Translation: Beware
of the dog)

CAVE C ANEM

Ruins at Pompeii

Acropolis, Athens

Beginnings In Greece

In 1764 the English Society of Dilettanti sent out the first organized expedition in the history of archaeology. Its three members went to Greece, and published a report on their return.

Greece was a favorite hunting ground for the antiquity collectors of the eighteenth and nineteenth centuries. For a long time it was under Turkish rule and nothing whatsoever was done to protect its monuments. The Parthenon, Athena's temple at Athens, had been used by the Turks as a gunpowder storehouse, and during a siege in the seventeenth century had been almost destroyed by a shell. Lord Elgin, British Ambassador to Turkey in the early nineteenth century, collected many of the Parthenon sculptures which might otherwise have been lost through further carelessness. The "Elgin Marbles," now in the British Museum, are considered among the most beautiful sculptures in the world.

Pyramids and Sphinx at Giza

Beginnings In Egypt

In 1798 Napoleon, Emperor of France, set sail to conquer Egypt. With him sailed a shipload of antiquarians who sketched and measured, and collected all the movable antiquities they could find.

After Napoleon's visit more antiquarians descended on Egypt, smashing their way into monuments, blasting them open, fighting each other like gangsters over the antiquities they carried off.

Just outside Cairo was a well-known "wonder of the world" too big to carry off: the three Pyramids of Giza, tombs of Pharaohs who ruled Egypt 4,500 years ago. One hundred thousand slaves had toiled for twenty years to build the Great Pyramid of King Cheops. Its huge stones were dragged from river barges and hoisted into place entirely by hand. The cost was the equivalent of many millions of dollars and countless human lives. The king's dead body was secretly placed in the heart of the pyramid, and all passages, entrances, and shafts were blocked so that he might

14

be undisturbed for ever and ever. But grave-robbing had been a profession in Egypt since earliest times. When the archaeologist Flinders Petrie explored the pyramid in 1880, he found the coffin empty and the king's treasures gone.

Luckily, with the growth of archaeology people began to realize how wrong it was to rob the ancient ruins, and there began a period of careful excavation by archaeologists of many lands which continues to this day.

The Prehistory Of Europe

In the nineteenth century, relics of prehistoric man were being turned up in Europe everywhere from Scandinavia to Spain. Caves, ancient rubbish heaps, remains of shellfish feasts, peat bogs, river beds, lake bottoms, all yielded their share of human skulls, bones, and tools. While setting up an exhibition for the Copenhagen Museum in 1836, Christian Thomsen worked out a plan for classifying settlements according to the material from which their tools were made: the *Three Age System*. It has been used as a framework for archaeology ever since.

The classifications are the *Age of Stone* (later divided into the *Old Stone Age* and the *New Stone Age*); the *Age of Bronze;* and the *Age of Iron.* The ages overlap, for often warriors used bronze weapons while common tools were still made of stone. The Three Age System is no guide to exact dates, for people reached different stages of development at different times. There are people in the world today who are still, or were till very recently, living at a Stone Age level.

Diagram of a cave, showing layers of occupation

Present floor

Iron tools

Bronze tools

Stone tools

Original cave bottom

Detective Story: Where to Dig

Ruins that could be seen, such as the Greek temples and the Egyptian pyramids, were the first sites to be explored. The archaeologists soon realized, however, that much, much more was hidden, and that they must become sleuths to find it. But the antiquarians had probably destroyed hundreds of clews of greatest value.

Even Botta and Layard, the amateurs, knew that a mound which somehow looked different from a natural hill should be investigated. The Near East is full of such mounds, called after the Arabic name for them: *tells.* It is quite easy to spot a "tell" by the way it rises suddenly from the plain: by its even shape and flat top, caused by the old wall that kept the rubble inside from washing away.

Mud and unbaked mud-bricks were the earliest and most common building material in the Near East. Both crumble if they get too wet during the rainy season. When a house collapsed, its owner leveled it off and built a new one on top of the crumbled material. Sometimes the town was destroyed by war, earthquake, or flood. The first settlers had come to this place for a special reason: because it had a spring of good water, or was on a caravan route, or a harbor for ships, or a hill easily defended. So after a disaster — sometimes many years after — men came to settle again in the same place for the same reason. They built new houses on the layer of soil that had drifted over the old ruins, or they used the rubble for foundations. And so, layer by layer, the tell grew higher until finally the space at the top was too small for a real town.

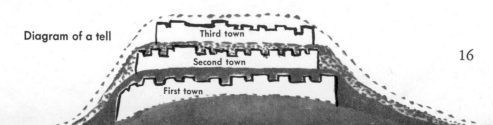

Diagram of a tell

Third town

Second town

First town

16

This tell, at Tepe Gawra,
has 26 layers of occupation
(from a photograph by Dr. E. A. Speiser)

In Egypt, temples were of stone, kept in good repair, while the common houses, of mud-brick, were constantly being rebuilt. The temple eventually lay in a hollow, and the clew to a lost temple, therefore, is a square depression surrounded by crumbling bricks.

There are small surface signs to watch for. Only a trained eye can recognize crude flint tools as different from natural stones. But *potsherds* — bits of shattered pottery — are easier to spot. There were no rubbish collectors in early days; people simply threw their broken dishes into the street or over the wall. And there they remain to this day, for though dishes are breakable, their pieces last almost forever.

Marked bricks poking up through the soil set Botta to digging at Kuyunjik.

17

Many accidental finds are reported, perhaps by workmen clearing ground for buildings and roads, or by farmers plowing their fields. Or a person may try to sell a find, and the news gets around. A trail of stolen antiquities offered for sale led to long-lost tombs in Egypt's Valley of the Kings.

Wars play their part. Roman remains appeared beneath the London streets when the bombing wreckage of World War II was cleared away. Military surveys made from planes have spotted unsuspected sites all over the world. Nowadays air surveys are made for purely archaeological reasons. A telescopic lens on an air camera spots things the eye cannot detect: very slight ridges or soil changes; crops that grow less high where roots are cramped by the ruins beneath them. Even at eye level or from a hill such clews can sometimes be seen. The patterns of ancient foundations or cemeteries which are invisible at noon may show up dramatically in the long shadows of sunset.

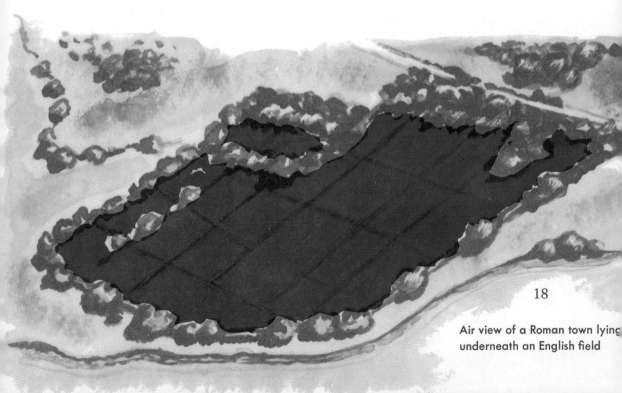

18

Air view of a Roman town lying underneath an English field

Some Accidental Finds

In Lascaux, France, two boys climbed down into a hole after their lost dog and found a prehistoric cave marvelously painted with pictures of extinct animals.

Painting from the Lascaux cave

The inscription on this little figure reads, "I am Lamgimari . . . King of Mari."

A strange statue, turned up by a Syrian villager, led to the excavation of Mari, one of the oldest cities in the world. This little statuette was found in the digging.

A poor woman, grubbing for fertilizer along the banks of the Nile, found some broken clay tablets which proved to be the letters of the Pharaoh Akhenaton. Highly important in themselves, they were also the clew to Akhenaton's city at Tell el 'Amarna, where excavations are still going on.

19

The head of Queen Nefertiti, found in a sculptor's studio at Tell el 'Amarna

Underwater archaeology has been helped enormously by the recent techniques of skin-diving: the swimming fins and aqua-lung, and enclosed waterproof cameras. Beneath the water lie ships sunk in battle, such as the Roman warships dredged up from Lake Nemi in Italy. Ships wrecked by storms have been reached, and their cargoes hoisted to the surface. The port and roadstead of ancient Tyre were surveyed by using divers, cameras, and glass-bottomed buckets. In the future, divers may reach more than one lost town which was overwhelmed when the land sank and the water rose. The contents of shipwrecks alone make the sea the greatest of all treasuries.

The archaeologist-detective must listen as well as look — listen to legends told by natives and for place names which sound like those of vanished cities. Arab stories of "Tell Jezar" led to the site of Gezer, the town that was the dowry of King Solomon's Egyptian bride. The Bible has been the guide to many excavations. There are clews to be found in old maps, Arab geographies, the accounts of early travelers, and very old books.

Undersea archaeology

From a Greek vase painting

Priam's Treasure

Heinrich Schliemann made a great discovery because of his interest in the oldest book in European literature, Homer's *Iliad*, written about 800 B.C. Schliemann's father had told him stories from this book almost as soon as the boy could talk — stories of the Greek siege of Troy. When he was seven years old, Heinrich said to his father, "One day I shall excavate Troy."

He taught himself Greek, worked his way up from a mean little job to an independent fortune, retired at the age of forty-six, and set out to discover Troy.

21

The Plain of Troy did exist in Asia Minor, but few scholars of the time believed the city of Troy to be more than a legend. Those who did think Troy real believed it had once stood on a hill called Bournabashi. Schliemann disagreed with them, arguing from such lines as these in the *Iliad*.

> Achilles started off in hot pursuit, and, like the dove flying before her enemy, Hector fled before him under the walls of Troy, fast as his feet could go . . . They sped along the cart track, and so came to the two lovely springs that are the sources of Scamander's eddying stream. In one of these the water comes up hot . . . But the other, even in summer, gushes up cold as hail . . .

Schliemann had stumbled and slipped on Bournabashi's rocky heights himself, and he knew that this was no place for flying feet; there was no room for a cart track, no hot spring or cold spring. He picked a hill called Hissarlik, closer to the sea, as fitting Homer's description, and began to dig there with his young Greek wife Sophia and some hired laborers. Almost at once their spades struck against the foundations of walls and towers, some of them scorched by fire.

22

Gold vessels and jewels from "Priam's treasure" (Schliemann)

Schliemann dug at Hissarlik for three seasons, going down and down into older and older cities — for there was not one Troy on this mound, but nine. Finally, one hot day at the end of the third season, he gave the order to quit for good. Suddenly he spied the gleam of metal at the bottom of a pit under the walls. A fugitive fleeing from the burning city had dropped a load of precious things. Schliemann called it the treasure of Priam, the Trojan king of whom Homer wrote. We know now that the city where Schliemann found the treasure was far older than Troy of the *Iliad*.

Later Schliemann excavated graves he thought to be those of Agamemnon and other Homeric heroes at Mycenae on the Greek mainland. The fact that these people lived several hundred years earlier than Agamemnon makes Schliemann's discoveries even more exciting. He had dug up the Mycenaeans, a people whose very existence had not even been suspected, yet who had lived in great palaces, worn fine jewels and flashing bronze armor, and had feasted from gold and silver dishes of fantastic beauty.

Golden mask, goblets, and sword from graves at Mycenae

(University Museum, Philadelphia)

Civilization In Layers: *Stratigraphy*

Schliemann, working in the last quarter of the nineteenth century, was the last of the great amateurs. He was also the first archaeologist to dig out a city-mound layer by layer. This method had been used before only in the study of geology and in a few simple small digs. Thomas Jefferson, in fact, was the first to use the method archaeologically, when he dug out an Indian burial and noted down the layers of earth, bones, and stones.

Often a digger will explore a site first by making a trial trench, slicing down through a mound as if it were a cake. On the fresh-cut sides of his trench he can see differences in color, different building materials, traces of fire or flood, holes made by posts that have rotted away, and any number of other hints to the history of the site. Wherever man has disturbed the soil, a scar remains.

Now, if the site looks promising and there are time and money for a thorough job, real excavation begins and is recorded layer by layer — a method of study called *stratigraphy*. Each layer, or *stratum*, was once a settlement with a certain *culture* — that is, a certain way of living. Each level is a page out of a history book, and, as with such a book, its pages must be read in correct order if the story of this particular place is to be learned. If the levels have not been mixed up by deep plowing or some other disturbance, the objects found just above bare earth or rock are the oldest, and those above it are newer and newer till you reach the top. It is like a pile of things on a table: the one at the bottom was put down first. There are some exceptions to watch for: old objects which have been inherited by later folk (like your great-grandmother's chair in your modern house); newer objects that have dropped down, through a pit perhaps, to an older level.

A dig, excavated
by the grid method
(see page 26)

One Day On A Dig: *Excavation*

Suppose that an archaeologist who is the director of a dig invites you to help. In the early morning before it is hot you climb the steep sides of a mound swarming with workers, assistants, students. Hired laborers, chanting as they work, are carrying basketfuls of waste soil to a train of small open cars. When it is full, the train clanks off to a dump.

The top of the mound looks like a huge brown waffle. It has been pegged out with string into numbered squares which correspond to squares drawn on a map of the site. Shallow pits are dug in each square. The raised bars of earth between them look like a

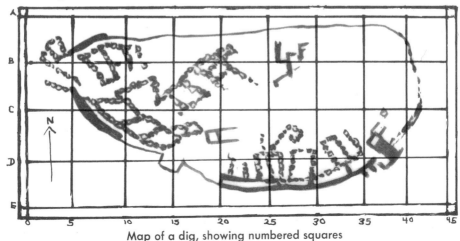

Map of a dig, showing numbered squares

Working on a dig

gridiron, hence this is called the *grid* method of excavating. The director gives you a mason's trowel or a small hand pick and tells you to dig out a pit about ten inches deep. You must keep the sides straight and neat; you must work with enormous patience, tapping the earth gently so as not to break the most fragile object. There are plums in this cake: pottery and other *artifacts* — articles made by man. When you come to one, you must lay aside your tool and use a finer one: a knife or an ice pick. (Sophia Schliemann explored a spot at Mycenae for twenty-five days with just her fingers and a pocketknife.) You must keep everything you find for a professional archaeologist to see — at least till you have some experience on a dig. Before the basket-carriers take away the soil you have loosened, you must look through it for any tiny thing you may have missed: a bead, a pierced sea shell, specks of metal, a tooth, a pin. When these are present, all the soil from the pit must

TOOLS USED IN EXCAVATING

Spade

Hand picks

Knife

Ice pick

Graduated triangle with bubble levels attached

Notebook with graph paper

Bubble level

Plumb bob

Turf cutter

be run through a wire-meshed sieve lest a single speck of evidence be lost.

All your finds go into boxes (the tiny ones into matchboxes) labeled with the number of your pit. At the end of the day the boxes will be collected and taken back to expedition headquarters. If something rare turns up while you are digging — a whole pot, for instance, or an image — you must call the director, because it might be broken by your inexpert handling. You watch him pry it out slowly and patiently, clearing away the loosened earth with a soft brush as he works, so that he knows just where to apply his tool next. He lays a measuring stick beside the treasure to show its size, and orders a photographer to take its picture 'in situ' (as it was found). Then he delicately lifts it from the bed where it has been sleeping for thousands of years, blows the dust from it, and cleans it with jewelers' tools.

Measuring poles

Tape measure

27

Two-foot rule

Sieve

Brushes

Basket

Pick

In another part of the mound experienced workmen with picks are following the lines of foundations and walls. The director orders the men to clear away the raised sections of the grid, so that the plan of the buildings can be traced. Students brush the walls clean; an assistant measures them with surveying instruments; the photographer takes pictures of them; and the architectural assistant draws them in on a chart of the site. Every find is marked on a plan and cross section so that it can be put back in position should the mound be restored. All excavation is destruction, though it is destruction with a purpose. This layer must be destroyed in order to explore the one beneath it. Only if everything is recorded will nothing be lost. The director will, however, leave part of the mound untouched, for future diggers to tackle, for he knows that digging methods are constantly improving.

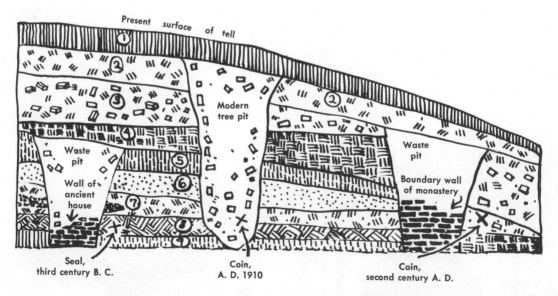

Cross section of a city mound, showing layers (from Wheeler)

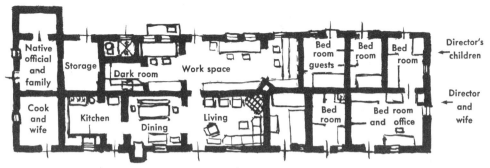

Native official and family | Storage | Dark room | Work space | Bed room guests | Bed room | Bed room | Director's children

Cook and wife | Kitchen | Dining | Living | Bed room | Bed room and office | Director and wife

Jarmo Expedition House

Expedition Headquarters: *Dealing with Finds*

The staff members of an expedition may live in tents, in native huts, a reroofed ruined palace, or a specially built house with such comforts as a refrigerator and showers. (Excavation is a hot and dusty business.) The well-equipped HQ has its own workshops, pottery shed, drafting room, darkroom for developing photographs, and storage space with many shelves.

Here the staff members clean, sort, and record the finds, and at the end of a strenuous day they eagerly discuss the meaning of what they have found.

One person picks up a jawbone. "This was a pig," he says. "But was it wild or domesticated?"

The jawbone and other bones will be packed in cotton wool to be sent to a zoologist, who will be able to tell the archaeologist what animals the people of this settlement kept in their homes, hunted, and ate.

Human bones may mean sacrifice to the gods, but more likely they mean a grave.

The dried particles in the bottom of a jar will be sent to a botanist to find out what grains and fruits were used for food.

The pierced sea shell, if this is an inland site, proves that the people of the settlement traded with others who lived on the coast.

29

Fitting together
an ancient pottery jar

Tracing trade routes in this way has proved that ancient communities were not nearly so isolated from each other as we used to think. The Greeks of Homer's tales, for instance, traded for amber as far north as Denmark, and got tin from Great Britain.

The arrows of hunters, the hooks and net sinkers of fishermen, the hoes and sickles of farmers, all add their bit to the life story of this site.

Potsherds are the commonest find. In the pottery shed these are carefully washed, or, if too fragile for that, they are cleaned with a soft brush. (An old toothbrush is handy for such a job.) Sometimes there are just too many sherds to save them all, so only rims, bases, spouts, handles, and decorated pieces are kept. These are the parts that show what the pottery was like before it was broken. Certain bits and pieces can often be fitted together like a jigsaw puzzle, and cemented into place. Thus a whole jar, or a large part of one, is reborn.

Seated at long tables, students match sherds to a color chart on the wall. They test the pieces for hardness and brittleness by pulverizing a corner with a hammer, or by biting and tasting them (but this is not considered scientific). Then comes the long job of

BONE NEEDLE   10
North Hill
Sq. A. Brown Clay
S.H.P. 1. 5
25. 7. 57

Find
card

T. Smith

30

marking a code number on each find with pen and India ink, and entering it in a catalogue with its code description, and the place and date of its discovery. A skilled draftsman makes an exact drawing to scale of the find. At the close of the expedition the director will publish his records, illustrated with pictures, for other archaeologists to study.

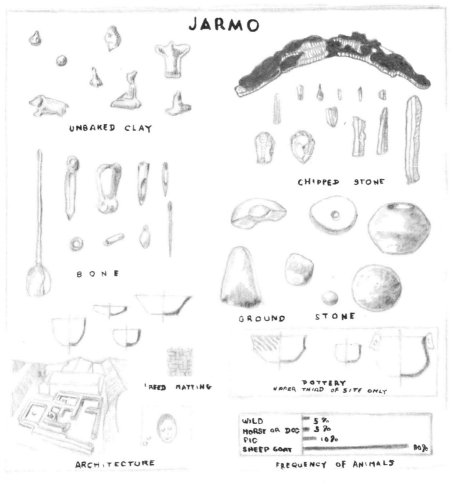

Sketches of Jarmo antiquities (from Braidwood)

From Petrie: One type of Egyptian prehistoric pottery

Why Pottery Is Important: *Typology*

In many parts of the world men discovered quite early that clay mud could be molded into pots. Later they found that if the pots were baked at a high temperature they would hold liquids, as baskets did not. The next step was to make the pots good to look at, as well as useful.

In ancient times, as in our own, people were constantly breaking their dishes and replacing them with the latest style — a fact of great use in dating. Because it was cheap, pottery was seldom imported or carried off as booty. Pottery is so valuable to modern archaeology just because it was of so little value to the ancients.

An archaeologist is trained to recognize the fine points that mark out the pottery of one people from the pottery of another, or set apart the pottery of the same people at different times. The archaeologist looks for differences in form and finish; and for the answers to these questions. Was the pot shaped by hand or on a wheel? How was it fired — that is, baked? How was it decorated?

Prehistoric hand axes (from Pitt-Rivers)

32

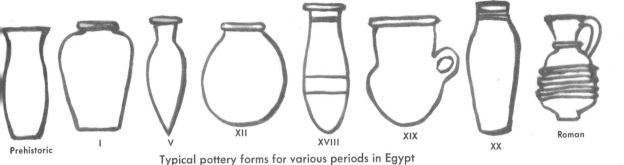

Prehistoric   I   V   XII   XVIII   XIX   XX   Roman

Typical pottery forms for various periods in Egypt

When he has found a jar in the oldest layer of a site, and a similar but slightly different jar in the next layer, and so forth, an archaeologist can set up a pottery *sequence:* a series that shows how the pottery of the site is developing. This sequence makes a sort of timetable for comparing the age of settlements in that part of the country.

Pottery sequences are a branch of *typology:* a method of study in which similar objects are arranged to show how one form grew out of another. General Pitt-Rivers, who collected all sorts of common things — tools, guns, clothing — and arranged them in sequences, said that progress was like a game of dominoes: like things fit to like; one domino follows another in orderly succession.

To an archaeologist a blackened bit of broken pottery clay means the man who made the pot, the woman who cooked in it, the children who ate from it. All the patient and sometimes tiresome work performed in a digging trench and a pottery shed brings to us who are alive the voices of these long-dead people.

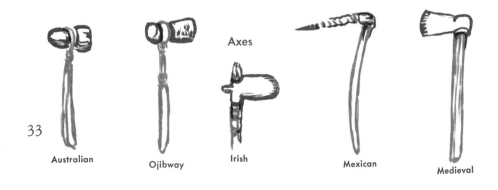

Axes

Australian   Ojibway   Irish   Mexican   Medieval

Chapters In The Story Of Man

The Three Age System classifies sites according to the tools found in them. The entire history of man, however, can be divided into three stages which are marked by big steps on the ladder of progress.

1. When savage man emerged from his animal ancestors, there were few of his kind among the beasts that roamed the earth. He had no horns or claws with which to defend himself or kill for food, but he had a clever brain. He invented weapons, tools, and language. He wandered about with his family, as animals do, and lived by hunting and gathering wild seeds, fruits, and roots. His bones have turned up in many parts of the world, and also his crude stone tools, which classify this period as the *Paleolithic (Old Stone) Age.*

2. Probably about eight thousand years ago, man discovered farming: how to tame animals and plant wild seeds. Then, apparently in the Near East, he settled for the first time in villages. Jarmo, in Iraq, is between six and seven thousand years old. The polished tools of this period give it the name *Neolithic (New Stone) Age.*

3. Civilization: By *civilization* we generally mean a culture, or way of life, which includes a government, a body of law, organized projects such as roads and industries. Two major inventions usually, but not always, accompanied these advances: writing and metallurgy — the extraction of metal from ore, and the making of metal tools, at first copper and bronze, and then iron. Civilization was born in the Near East for the first time anywhere on earth about five thousand years ago when the cities of Sumer rose in the valley of the Tigris and Euphrates Rivers (Mesopotamia — modern Iraq); and a little later, in the valley of the Nile (Egypt), and the Indus (modern Pakistan). In two other parts of the world, China and Central America, great civilizations rose independently, but at a considerably later date. We ourselves are living in the Third Chapter of the Book of Man and, it is sometimes said, in the *Atomic Age.*

How Old Is It? *Chronology*

Pottery sequences help to tell how old one site is as compared with another. Coins bearing dates are more exact, but coinage was not invented till some time between 800 and 500 B.C.

For exact dates an archaeologist must look to history, which includes the ancient written records that modern scholars have learned to read. The Egyptians and the Mesopotamians kept lists of their kings, with the length of each reign. Kings put their names on victory monuments; and builders of temples put theirs on foundation stones. Thus the date of the victory was fixed, and the age of the temple. The king lists were not always accurate, but in connection with certain events many ancient people wrote down the movements of sun, moon, and stars. From these observations our astronomers can figure out quite exact dates. The most important single date is June 15, 763 B.C., the day of a full eclipse of the sun in the region of Nineveh. This event was noted in a list of 250 annual entries, and as a result events from about 900 to 650 B.C. both in Assyrian and Biblical history have been accurately dated. So, bit by bit, one event in ancient history is linked to another.

A stone from the temple of the Egyptian Queen Hatshepsut. On the left is the name of the queen's architect and the date, about 1475 B. C.

35

(Metropolitan Museum)

The victory monument of Naram-sin, King of Akkad, about 2650 B. C.

(Musée du Louvre)

When an archaeologist tackles a new site, he first of all reads all there is to know of it in written records, new and old. If there are no records, he calls in experts to deal with his finds.

Through the ages, changes of climate have left their traces in soil, rock, and vegetable remains. Human remains found in the gravel beds left by the retreating glaciers of the last Ice Age, for instance, can be dated by a geologist.

Plant pollen cannot be destroyed, and is easily identified under a microscope. An expert botanist knows when certain plants grew in certain parts of the world, and so he dates a site.

A paleontologist knows when the kinds of animals painted on a cave wall finally died out.

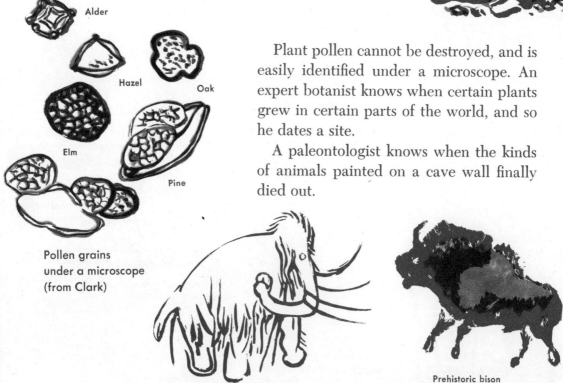

Alder

Hazel

Oak

Elm

Pine

Pollen grains
under a microscope
(from Clark)

Extinct mammoth

Prehistoric bison

Figures from French cave paintings

All material that has once been alive contains an element called *carbon-14,* which is radioactive: that is, it has the power to give off a certain type of energy. But it loses this power at a known rate after death. A splinter of wood or bone, a bit of charcoal, a shred of reed matting, can be tested for the radioactivity of its carbon-14, and mathematics will give its approximate age.

In the American Southwest the annual growth rings of trees form a pattern, with differences caused by wet seasons and dry seasons. A *series* has been set up by matching the inner pattern of a younger tree to the outer pattern of an older tree, all the way back to where the patterns match those of beams from early Indian settlements. Since each ring represents a year, a fairly accurate date for the settlement can be figured out.

These are only some of the methods of *fixing a chronology,* that is, of calculating how old things are when no historical dates are known.

Matching rings from a series of trees of different ages

37

Puzzle Pages For Scholars: *Deciphering Texts*

Most early records were inscribed on stone or clay. The Egyptians invented papyrus, a paperlike material made from river reeds. When the Egyptian papyrus records were first discovered by Europeans, no one could read them.

The key to Egyptian writing was a black basalt slab, the Rosetta stone, discovered by one of Napoleon's officers. Three columns of script were inscribed on the stone: one was *hieroglyphs*, or picture symbols; the second was a simpler, but still unknown, writing that grew from hieroglyphs; and the third was in Greek letters.

Most of those who were trying to decipher hieroglyphs thought

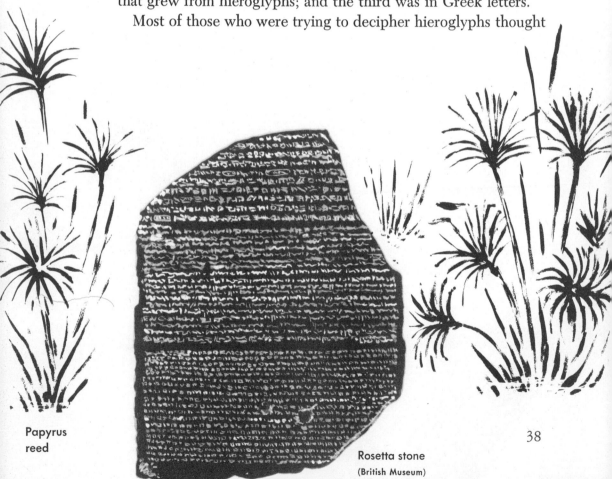

Papyrus
reed

Rosetta stone
(British Museum)

38

that they were pictures, as if 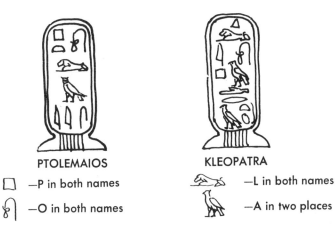 was the word for lion; was the word for hawk; was the word for water. Jean Jacques Champollion, a brilliant young French scholar, realized that Egyptian writing had advanced from this earliest stage to symbols which represented sounds. (represents the sound we know as N.)

In addition to the Rosetta stone, Champollion studied the Greek and hieroglyphic inscriptions on an *obelisk,* or monument of an Egyptian king, Ptolemy, and the queen, Cleopatra. Certain groups

PTOLEMAIOS

☐ —P in both names

—O in both names

KLEOPATRA

—L in both names

—A in two places

of hieroglyphs were set off by an oval ring, or *cartouche.* Scholars had guessed that only royalty would be so honored, and an Englishman, Dr. Thomas Young, had discovered the hieroglyphs for Ptolemy and Cleopatra. Starting with these, Champollion worked out the alphabetic sounds for twelve hieroglyphic symbols. Then it was possible to arrive at the others, including earlier hieroglyphs which did not represent alphabetic letters, but syllables and words.

The Egyptians probably got the *idea* for writing, man's greatest invention, from the Sumerians of Lower Mesopotamia. The oldest written material so far discovered is from the Sumerian city of Uruk, dating from before 3000 B.C. The writing of Mesopotamia is called *cuneiform,* which means "wedge-shaped," because it was inscribed on tablets of soft clay by an instrument — at first probably a sharpened reed — which left wedge-shaped impressions.

The key to cuneiform was a triple inscription on a monument of King Darius of Persia, carved on the great Rock of Behistun. When a young Englishman, Lieutenant Henry Rawlinson, went to Persia as a military adviser in 1835, he risked his life many times to copy the inscriptions, which later proved to be Old Persian, Elamite, and Babylonian. He brought ladders, and dangled from ropes four hundred feet above the valley floor, but he could not get close enough to copy one inscription (the Babylonian). Twelve years later he found a native boy who climbed like a cat, hanging on by fingers and toes, to make a *squeeze* — a cast in wet pulped paper. Recently a University of Michigan professor made a squeeze of the same inscription, using the latest material: rubber latex.

Dudu, a Sumerian scribe of about 2350 B.C.

Picture writing on a tablet from Ur, about 2000 B. C.

(University Museum, Philadelphia)

40

"King Darayawaush gives notice thus:
You who in future days
Will see this inscription by order
Writ with hammer upon the cliff
Who will see these human figures here—
Efface, destroy nothing.
Take care, so long as you have seed,
To leave them undisturbed."
    —Inscription of King Darius on the Rock of Behistun

Rawlinson did not know of Grotefend, a German who had already deciphered some cuneiform characters from copies of Persian texts. Rawlinson, however, used the same method as Grotefend, working out the Old Persian from the names of known Persian kings and their titles. Later he and others deciphered the two older languages, Elamite and Babylonian, with the help of "dictionaries" inscribed on clay tablets found in the "library" of Sennacherib's palace at Nineveh. So was solved the enormous puzzle

41

Dog

Bread

Earth

Beer

Spade

Earliest picture writing signs, about 3100 B. C.

Ox

of a writing used for many different languages, in which the same symbol can stand for a word, a syllable, a letter, or for several different words or syllables. Here are words from a tablet written by a Sumerian schoolboy about four thousand years ago.

> When I awoke early in the morning, I faced my mother and said to her, "Give me my lunch. I want to go to school . . ." In school the monitor in charge said to me, "Why are you late?"

Garden

Writing developed gradually from pictures of objects to symbols for syllables and words. Then the next great step was an alphabet. The earliest alphabetic writing so far found is on tablets of the fourteenth century B.C., dug up at Ugarit, in Syria. This alphabet, handed on to the Phoenicians and the Hebrews, and then through the Greeks and Etruscans to the Romans, is the ancestor of ours. The letters of our alphabet remain in the very same order as was used at Ugarit.

There are still some unsolved puzzles among ancient writings. Only a little is known of the language of the Etruscans, who developed a rich civilization in Italy before the Romans.

Canal

Of the three kinds of ancient Cretan script, only one, called "Linear B," has been deciphered, very recently, by a young English architect, Michael Ventris. It has proved to be a very old form of Greek.

How cuneiform developed

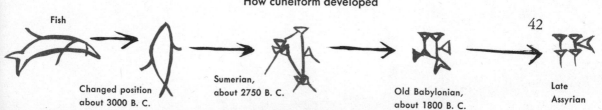

Fish

Changed position about 3000 B. C.

Sumerian, about 2750 B. C.

Old Babylonian, about 1800 B. C.

Late Assyrian

42

Some Mesopotamian "Firsts" Which We Have Inherited

Libraries: In the palace of Sennacherib and his grandson Ashurbanipal at Nineveh, thousands of clay tablets were found, many of them plainly copies of older works: stories, dictionaries, medical works with prescriptions for drugs, tablets on botany, chemistry, and astronomy.

The oldest library catalogue, about 2000-1300 B. C.

Mathematics: Sumerian arithmetic was based on the numbers 60 and 10. We have inherited our way of telling time from this, and our division of the circle into 360 degrees. The Sumerians knew how to use fractions and to extract square roots.

Law: Ur-Nammu, king of Sumer and Akkad in about 2100 B.C., drew up what is probably the earliest real law code. The code of Hammurabi, King of Babylon from about 1955 to 1913 B.C., was inscribed on a stone for all to see: laws regulating property, banking, wills, marriage, child adoption, army service, liquor consumption, and crime. Bible law was later than this code and much like it.

Stone tablet, with the code of Hammurabi

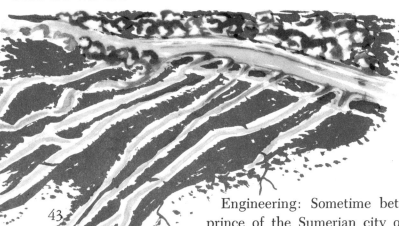

43

Engineering: Sometime between 3000 and 2000 B.C. a prince of the Sumerian city of Lagash built the first irrigation canals. The Iraq government is trying to restore these to bring the country back to its former prosperity.

Canals in Iraq

The Dead Tell Their Story: *Evidence from Graves*

Graves are favored sites for diggers: archaeologists probably learn more about a people from their burial customs than from anything else. Most ancient people buried their dead with offerings. The Egyptians carried this custom to an extreme. Two kinds of people unexpectedly benefited from it: tomb robbers and archaeologists.

The Egyptians believed that a man's soul must be supplied after death with everything he had ever needed in life. A rich man took with him into his tomb his clothes, jewels, furniture, dishes, food, and drink. Slaves to care for him were modeled in wood and in clay and set beside him — grooming his horses, baking bread, brewing beer. On the tomb walls were scenes from his daily life, painted with the hope that he would continue to enjoy such activities after death: pictures of him hunting and fishing; feasting,

44

Egyptian tomb painting

Boat model,
found in an Egyptian tomb

with musicians and dancers to amuse him; sailing down the Nile in his boat, with fish swimming beneath it and birds flying overhead. His wife combs her hair, attended by maidservants, or she plays with her children and her pets. His laborers work in the fields, drive cows and spotted calves and little long-eared donkeys. Butchers cut up meat; bricklayers build houses; potters mix clay. There is scarcely an occupation that is not pictured in some dead Egyptian's tomb.

Egypt's Greatest Treasure

Tut-Ankhamen was a pharaoh who died at eighteen after an unimportant life spent mostly in designing a gorgeous tomb for himself. Howard Carter and Lord Carnarvon hunted for this tomb in the Valley of the Kings for six years and found the entrance to it, just as they were about to give up, on November 3, 1922. Carter took two seasons to clear the antechamber alone of gilded furniture, statues, boxes, and this golden, jewel-inlaid throne.

Throne of Tut-Ankhamen

In the inner chamber were four gold-plated shrines, nested like Chinese boxes. A stone casket enclosed three coffins, one inside the other. This innermost one, of solid gold, contained the king's body, which could hardly be seen for the gold and jewels which covered it. A tiny wreath of withered flowers — perhaps the gift of the pharaoh's young queen — lay on the gold mask that covered the face.

Modern archaeology succeeded where robbers failed, rescuing from the grave the incredibly beautiful things which the world would otherwise never have seen. Howard Carter's patience and skill brought them forth whole and unshattered. Now, in the Cairo Museum, two guards stand with their hands on their revolvers day and night, watching over King Tut-Ankhamen's burial gifts whose value is so great that it cannot be calculated.

46

Gold coffin of Tut-Ankhamen

The Woolley expedition clearing the graves at Ur (from a photograph, Woolley)

Reviving Ghosts: *The Preservation of Finds*

An Egyptian's body was mummified — treated with ointments and wrappings so it would not decay after death. But what really preserved it for us to see was the dry, clean desert air that preserved also the fine linen clothes and bedding, the wooden tables and chairs. All these might have rotted away in the damp soil of some other countries.

Austen Layard, writing of Nineveh, reports sadly how, again and again, an object that was whole when first found, crumbled to dust as soon as it was touched. Nowadays first aid is given to a delicate object on the spot. It is coated with a preservative — partly acetate, like liquid nail polish — before it is moved. If necessary, it is lifted out still embedded in a block of earth.

Even things that have already vanished can be made to live again, as Leonard Woolley proved in his work at the Sumerian city of Ur, one of the oldest cities in the world. Woolley dug out hundreds of graves among the refuse heaps on the outskirts of the city-mound. The soil was salty and many of the wonderful finds were in bad shape. Woolley and his assistants spent "painful hours" stooping and lying over the skeletons, blowing and cutting away the soil from loose beads so that they might be photographed and later restrung in their right order.

A fine powdery streak showed that straw matting had once lined a grave. It had left an impression in the soil, and Woolley's photograph of the impression looks like the matting itself.

Hot wax and bandages, applied "in situ" to hundreds of bits of blue lapis lazuli and shell, rescued a mosaic panel which was cemented together again. This reborn "Royal Standard of Ur,"

The Royal Standard of Ur

meant to be carried like a flag, is for us an illustrated strip of the Sumerian customs of 4,500 years ago. The kings of Ur, unlike the later Assyrians, shaved their heads and beards. They wore tasseled skirts; received tribute of sheep, cattle, and goats; feasted to the music of harps; and went forth to war in four-wheeled chariots. This is the first appearance of a wheeled vehicle anywhere on earth.

48

Woolley saved dozens of precious things. A statuette of a ram, smashed almost flat, was carefully pressed back into shape. A sledge chariot whose wooden parts had rotted away was reconstructed from its metal parts.

Woolley found a mystery, however, whose meaning he could not reconstruct: mass burials — the bodies of men and women who had either been murdered or had meekly laid themselves down to follow their kings and queens into death. Ladies wore ropes of precious beads and crowns of gold leaves and jeweled flowers. Dead grooms lay at the heads of dead asses which were harnessed to sledge chariots decorated with gold, silver, and mosaic. Perhaps archaeologists will someday supply the explanation of these "Royal Graves of Ur."

49

Gaming board from Ur

Gold drinking tube from Ur

(University Museum,
Philadelphia)

Harp

The ziggurat of Ur
(from a restoration by Woolley)

Up From The Ashes: *Reconstructing Buildings*

According to the Bible, Abraham went forth from Ur to journey to the land of Canaan by way of Central Mesopotamia (Haran). From the remains of dwellings at Ur, Woolley had a picture drawn of a house as it must have looked in Abraham's time, about the nineteenth century B.C. Such reconstructions on paper are often part of expedition reports. They call for special architectural knowledge, as well as skill in draftsmanship.

A most elaborate example of actual rebuilding is the palace of Knossos in Crete. In 1894 the English archaeologist Arthur Evans arrived in Crete to excavate the rubble-strewn mound that Schliemann had picked as the site of the palace of Minos, legendary king of Crete. Here Evans discovered the remains of a rich, gay prehistoric people whom he named, for the king, Minoan.

The palace of Knossos was many-storied, with hundreds of passages, stairways, reception rooms, private apartments, and storage cellars filled with huge jars for wine and oil. It had plumbing: private bathrooms with toilets, drains, and running water — a luxury unknown for thousands of years thereafter. Evans, who was a rich man, restored some of the buildings at his own expense. He replaced with concrete the vanished colonnades of wood, judging their size and unusual shape from stone bases and capitals which had not burned or rotted away. He redecorated rooms according to the faded scraps of design still on the walls, and painted in the missing sections of frescoes.

51

Palace of Knossos
(as restored by Evans)

Wall painting of bull dancers, Knossos

New Light On Old Tales

One of the mural paintings at Knossos suggests the truth that may lie behind a famous legend. Athens, it was said, had to send seven youths and seven maidens every nine years to be sacrificed to a bull-like monster that lived at Knossos in a labyrinth — a maze of twisting passageways from which no one ever found his way out. But at last the Athenian prince Theseus killed the Minotaur and sailed home with Ariadne, daughter of Minos.

From 2000 to 1400 B.C., Crete was the greatest sea power in the Mediterranean. Its beautiful vases have been found in Greece, Syria, Egypt, and elsewhere. Very likely the Greeks were forced to send young people as hostages to the king of Knossos. The bull was a sacred animal in Crete: a wall painting shows youths and maidens somersaulting over a bull's back — a form of bullfighting which may have led to the Minotaur legend. The victory of Theseus may represent a Greek invasion and victory, for the ruins of Knossos show that it fell and was burned. And in Knossos's last days the "Linear B" inscriptions suddenly appear — inscriptions in

52

Greek similar to those found at Mycenae on the Greek mainland. Here is another kind of detective work: the piecing together of evidence which shows there is some truth in the old stories after all.

Another example is the Great Flood story. Mesopotamia is a land of many devastating floods, while mountainous Canaan, the land of the Bible, is not. The Sumerian epic of Gilgamesh, inscribed on clay tablets found in the Nineveh library, includes the story of a great flood. Ut-napishtim builds an ark, fills it with animals, floats on the waters for many days, sends forth a dove, and finally finds dry land. This is the origin of the Bible story of Noah and his ark.

And the great ziggurat at Babylon, a tall temple tower with setbacks like a modern skyscraper, is sometimes said to be the "tower of Babel."

Gilgamesh

The Flood Tablet

(University Museum,
Philadelphia)

The walls of Jericho

The Land Of The Bible

Almost every foot of ground in modern Israel and Jordan is full of relics, from cave remains to Crusader castles. Bible archaeology is a field in itself. Among the important discoveries are these.

When Joshua marched his besieging army, shouting and blowing on trumpets, seven times round Jericho, the walls came tumbling down. Excavation shows that part of the wall, though it was 25 feet high and 12 feet thick, did fall, perhaps from an earthquake, perhaps because its foundations were weak.

Megiddo and Hazor were two of King Solomon's fortress cities, where the stone hitching posts of his chariot stables have been found. So many battles were fought over the pass of Megiddo

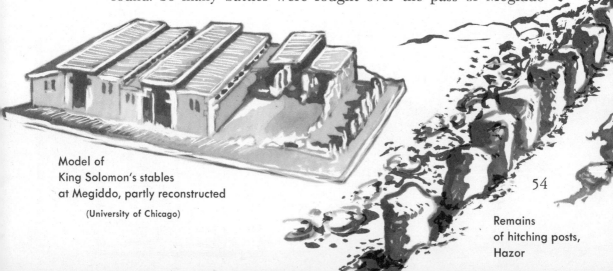

Model of
King Solomon's stables
at Megiddo, partly reconstructed

(University of Chicago)

54

Remains
of hitching posts,
Hazor

Ruins at Capernaum

(also called Armageddon) that, according to *Revelations,* the last great battle of the world, between the forces of good and evil, would be fought there. The last battle actually fought at Armageddon was between the British and the Turks in World War I.

At Ezion-geber, on the Red Sea, King Solomon built his "navy of Tharshish." The remains of shipyards and copper refineries have been excavated. Nearby are mines where you can still pick up burned ore from which Solomon's workmen extracted copper.

At Capernaum on the Sea of Galilee there stands a partly restored synagogue which was built in the third century on the foundations of one in which Jesus preached.

Jerusalem, the principal city of Palestine, is a holy city for Jews, Christians, and Moslems. Many people live there, and its houses cannot be destroyed for excavation purposes. But some work has been done on old walls, tunnels, and tombs which identify places mentioned in both the Old and the New Testaments.

Jerusalem

In 1947 a Bedouin boy tossed a stone into a cave in the desolate country near the Dead Sea. Upon investigating the sound of smashing, he found some old scrolls hidden in jars. Archaeologists followed up this discovery by excavating a nearby ruin, and found similar jars, and Roman coins dated from 31 B.C. to A.D. 67. Carbon-14 tests of the linen wrappings of the scrolls suggest an earlier date. Most scholars agree that the scrolls were written between the first century B.C. and the first century of our era.

The building was a monastery of a Jewish sect called the Essenes. It was burned when the Jews revolted against the Romans in A.D. 70. The scrolls must have been books from its library which were hidden just before this event. Among the Dead Sea scrolls, as they are called, are the oldest copies of the *Book of Isaiah* in existence. Other scrolls tell the rules and beliefs of the Essenes, which resemble the teachings of Jesus. They make a link between the Jewish and Christian religions. The job of unrolling the fragile scrolls and deciphering them is still going on — and so are the arguments among scholars which this exciting find has stirred up.

56

Dead Sea scrolls

Prehistoric Sites of North America

America was first discovered by Mongol tribesmen who crossed Bering Strait from Siberia to Alaska and drifted south to people the American continents. We know that men lived in the caves of North America 25,000 years ago, because bones of extinct animals — the mammoth, the giant sloth, the prehistoric horse and camel — have been found with the flint spear points that killed them.

Ruins at Mesa Verde

The Pueblo Indians of our Southwest are the direct descendants of the Anasazi (a Navaho name for the "Ancient Ones"), whose great period was from A.D. 1050 to 1300. The Anasazi built many-storied houses, each a whole town in itself, such as those at Mesa Verde, in Colorado, and Chaco Canyon, in New Mexico. These "apartment houses" were abandoned, probably because crops failed for want of rain, and their inhabitants moved to found the villages where their descendants live today.

The people in the Eastern United States before A.D. 900 built log tombs covered by cone-shaped earth mounds as much as seventy feet high. They buried their dead with stone axes and knives, copper bracelets, ear spools, helmets, breastplates; beads and necklaces of pearls.

Illinois mound-builders' regalia

Pottery from the mounds
of the Lower Mississippi Valley

Worship of the sun and other gods came into the Mississippi Valley from Mexico after A.D. 900. Hundreds of ceremonial centers, arranged about central courts in groups, were built of earth with log-faced stairways, in imitation of the stone pyramids of Middle America. From time to time the wooden temple on the flat top of each mound was burned, and a new one built.

Civilizations Of Central America

The Indians called Mayas were a civilized people when most Europeans were still barbarians. The examples of their picture-symbol writing which have been deciphered prove their genius at mathematics. The Mayas had a sign for zero long before our own 0 was brought from India in the eighth century. They had a calendar more exact than any but the one we use today.

0   1   2

3   4   5

Mayan picture symbols for numerals

During their great period, which probably lasted from A.D. 472 to a few hundred years before the Spanish conquest of Mexico in 1519, the Mayas built over a hundred cities in Yucatan, Honduras, and Guatemala. In 1839 an American, John Lloyd Stephens, was the first to clear the jungle from an abandoned city of the Mayas: Copán. His English artist-companion, Frederick Catherwood, copied the sculpture which covered every inch of the stairways, walls, and monuments: queer staring faces, feathered serpents, jaguars, and complicated designs.

Idol and altar, Copan, Honduras
(from Catherwood)

58

Mayan pyramids with temples

The Mayan temples stood on great stone pyramids, surrounded by houses for priests and lords; ball courts; and astronomical observatories. But the Mayan farming methods were primitive, and quickly exhausted the soil. When the city began to starve, the whole population had to leave it and build a new city elsewhere.

Many other Indian nations of Central America, some earlier than the Mayas, some later, were skilled craftsmen and master-architects. The Aztecs were a powerful warrior people whose religion demanded constant human sacrifice. Hated and feared by the other tribes over which they ruled, the Aztecs were conquered by the Spaniards, and with their downfall the great Central American Indian civilizations came to an end.

Snake head, Mexico

The Corn Spirit makes an offering (from a native drawing)

The most important food of the Indian civilizations of America was maize, or Indian corn; much of the religion, many of the customs, grew from the need to cultivate it successfully. We have inherited corn, popcorn, and corn bread from the Indians, and also rubber, rubber-soled sandals, rubber-proofed rain-capes, white potatoes, and avocados. *Chocolate*, *tobacco*, and *tomato* are Indian words for Indian plants. We did *not* adopt the Mayan bombs — hornets' nests which they threw at their enemies.

The Inca Empire

When the Spaniards reached South America in 1532, the Incas were a ruling class that controlled the fate of from three to six million people. In Cuzco, their capital city, the Temple of the Sun had gold-plated doors, walls, and pillars; fountains with golden pipes; statues and images of gold. This marked out the Incas as victims for Spanish greed; conquest was easy because the people had no real loyalty to their dictator-rulers.

Machu Picchu,
an Inca fortress

Pottery head
of an Inca soldier

The Inca roads ran from Cuzco to the four corners of the Empire, over mountains and deserts, crossing rivers and deep gorges by suspension bridges. After the conquest large sections of the Inca road were lost, but a recent expedition has retraced them. The country is so vast and so wild that excavators have only sampled the remains of the remarkable Inca cities.

The prehistoric Indians of South America were artists in metal and pottery. They were master-weavers who left behind beautiful gingham cloth, gauze, lace, and embroidery. They were good farmers, excellent architects and builders. They had no written language, but the Incas kept accounts and records on the *quipu*, a system of colored and knotted cords. In the Andes Mountains of Peru and Bolivia the Inca language and customs survive; even the same musical instruments are played: drums, copper bells, bone flutes, trumpets, and whistles.

The quipu

Why? The Purpose of Archaeology

Archaeology has come a long way from its beginnings in antiquity-collecting and treasure-hunting. Nor is the story ended. Methods of digging and studying finds are growing more scientific all the time; our knowledge is constantly increasing; our theories about early man are still changing. New finds may easily change some of our ideas even more. Archaeology is such a recent science that there is a great deal still to be done in it — a great deal that young archaeologists of the future will still give to it.

At times the question is asked, "What good is it?" Mortimer Wheeler, an eminent "digger" of today, says, "The archaeologist is digging up, not *things*, but *people* . . . Dead archaeology is the driest dust that blows." Archaeology tells us the history of men very much like ourselves. How much the "old ones" knew that we had thought to be new in the world! How many mistakes they made that we are making, too! Nations grew strong and then collapsed of their own tyranny; some civilizations handed on knowledge, and others vanished without leaving anything of importance. The Egyptians left behind great art; the Greeks left great art and also a way of thought from which stems much of the thinking of the modern Western world. A small weak group, the ancient Hebrews, gave us our great inheritance, the Bible.

We too are part of a stream of progress that began when man started to walk erect, make tools, and speak in words. There are lessons to be learned from the past. The men of the past made us what we are; we are making the future.

61

How To Become An Archaeologist

To be a full-fledged archaeologist these days takes knowledge and training which is offered at many universities. Archaeology is often listed in university catalogues with or under *Anthropology*, which is the study of man's development and his different beliefs and customs. Archaeology offers many kinds of work, from digging to classifying and setting up finds in museums. Digging methods are pretty much the same everywhere, from the Near East to New Mexico, but when it comes to the study of historical background and languages, a student does better to specialize on the part of the world that most interests him.

Then there are the related sciences and special skills that make those who know them always welcome among archaeologists: geology, zoology, botany, architecture, and other fields mentioned in this book. A recent large expedition included, besides the director and his assistants, the following staff members: architect, epigrapher (who reads inscriptions), surveyor, field chemist, artists

to copy frescoes and murals, supervisor for the restoration of buildings, photographer, trained housekeeper, and trained nurse.

A modern expedition may travel in jeeps instead of on mule-back, but there is still discomfort and sometimes danger in the remote places to which it goes. In spite of scientific methods, no one knows beforehand just what will turn up when the digging begins. Adventure is just around the corner — the adventure of discovering something no one ever knew before.

And *anyone* can make a discovery *anywhere*. The ancient world was, after all, the same earth on which we live today. A few years ago a thirteen-year-old boy discovered a cave with Indian remains a few miles from New York City. Anyone can learn, from museum collections and from books, what to look for. And then — keep your eyes open!

63

Index

For further reading

The Archaeologist at Work, by Clark Wissler. American Museum of Natural History, New York. 1953.

The Aztecs. Pan American Union, Washington, D.C. 1955.

The Building of Ancient Egypt, by Helen and Richard Leacroft. Puffin Picture Books, Penguin Books, Ltd.

The Home Life of the Ancient Egyptians, by Nora E. Scott. Metropolitan Museum of Art, New York.

The Incas. Pan American Union, Washington, D. C. 1955.

The Mayas. Pan American Union, Washington, D. C. 1954.